What to Expect
in Reformed Worship

What to Expect
in Reformed Worship

A Visitor's Guide

DANIEL R. HYDE

Second Edition

WIPF & STOCK · Eugene, Oregon

WHAT TO EXPECT IN REFORMED WORSHIP
A Visitors' Guide
Second Edition

Wipf & Stock
An Imprint of Wipf and Stock Publishers
199 W. 8th Ave., Suite 3
Eugene, OR 97401
www.wipfandstock.com

ISBN 13: 978-1-62032-795-1
Manufactured in the U.S.A.

Unless otherwise indicated, all Scripture quotations are from The Holy
Bible, English Standard Version ® (ESV ®), copyright © 2001 by Crossway,
a publishing ministry of Good News Publishers. Used by permission. All
rights reserved.

All citations of the Belgic Confession, Canons of Dort, and Heidelberg
Catechism are from The Creeds of Christendom: Volume 3, The Evangelical
Protestant Creeds, ed. Philip Schaff, rev. David S. Schaff (1931; repr., Grand
Rapids: Baker Books, 1996).

All citations of the Wesminster Confession, Shorter, and Larger Cat-
echisms are from Westminster Confession of Christendom (1958; repr.,
Glasgow, Scotland: Free Presbyterian Publications, 2009).

To all saints who have preserved the old paths of biblical, Christian, and Reformed worship, so that newcomers like me had something substantive to cling onto—so that newcomers can continue to cling to Christ through our services.

Contents

Preface to the Second Edition

"Oh, MAGNIFY THE LORD with me, and let us exalt his name together" (Ps. 34:3). I am so gratified that this little book you hold in your hands continues to be a source of instruction and inspiration to many, as together we worship the Lord. In updating it now as a second edition, I have kept the same structure and purpose of introducing the basics of our worship to those who are new to a Reformed church. In this second edition, though, I have updated the style since I have developed as a writer over the years. I have also expanded certain sections to give more clarity and depth as well as added a walking through a basic evening service. Finally, I have moved what used to be the last chapter on the minister's attire into an appendix. In doing this I intend this book to be more useable by more ministers and churches. The result, I pray, is that this work leads many more people to grow in their magnification and exaltation of our wonderful Triune God.

Abbreviations

BC—Belgic Confession

BCP—*Book of Common Prayer* (1662)

CD—Canons of Dort

HC—Heidelberg Catechism

WCF—Westminster Confession of Faith

WLC—Westminster Larger Catechism

WSC—Westminster Shorter Catechism

Introduction

As a new convert to Jesus Christ, I was zealous to worship the Lord every day and in every way. I showed up early on Sunday mornings, went to services and Bible studies during the week, sung in my car, sung in my dorm at college, read my Bible during lunchtime, talked about the Lord with family and friends, and listened to Christian pastors on the radio. Sadly, while I was "running well" with this zeal, I was soon "hindered" (Gal 5:1) by disillusionment in my first year at college. As a recent convert, I choose a Christian college because I thought that would build up my faith more than a big university. As a Christian college, we had required courses in Bible, theology, and church history, as well as three chapel services each week. What could be disillusioning about all this? Frankly, it all seemed empty. Friends and other students would party all weekend with alcohol, drugs, and sex, only to engage in the weekly ritual of "re-dedicating" their lives to the Lord during the altar call in chapel or "repent" to the campus pastor when caught. In response I ceased going to chapel and church. There was one thing, though, that eventually drew me out of this deep disappointment and time of questioning of my faith: the worship of a Reformed church. After hearing an advertisement for this church on Christian radio I was intrigued. When I attended, I found the depth I had been looking for. The service was reverent and joyful, the liturgy was saturated with Scripture, and the celebration of Holy Communion filled me with awe and comfort. I certainly did not know why things were done the way they were, when to stand and when to sit, or even how to sing out of a hymnal, but what I did know was that there was something in that worship service that was real—and I desperately needed it.

That something was biblically ordered and heartfelt worship of the Triune God of grace. Over the next few years I learned that we all exist as humans "to glorify God, and to enjoy him forever" (WSC, Q&A 1). Our entire lives are to be devoted to worshipping God with our entire heart, soul, and mind (Matt 22:37). And this worship comes to its culmination when a congregation gathers publicly to say, "I was glad when they said to me, 'Let us go to the house of the Lord!'" (Ps 122:1)[1]

Yet, I also learned that we do not exist to worship our Creator in isolation (Heb 10:25). In the beginning, the God who exists eternally in community as Father, Son, and Holy Spirit, said, "Let *us* make man" (Gen 1:26). The text of Scripture then says, "So God created man in his own image, in the image of God he created him; male and female he created *them*" (Gen 1:27). God created us out of, into, and for community. Adam, though, on behalf of all humanity, rejected this purpose when he sinned by rebelling against his Creator (Gen 3:1–6; Rom 5:12–21). Not only did Adam reject his purpose to glorify God, his sin made all humanity incapable of offering true worship. God is so amazing, though. In response, he served the creature! Scripture says that God came to Adam and Eve, hiding from his Maker among the trees, and clothed them with animal skins, a visible sign to them that he covered their sins (Gen 3:7–8, 21). God's serving his people in grace led to their response. While the communities of the world made names for themselves in city-building, animal domestication, music, and metallurgy (Gen 4:17–22), the community of faith gathered, to "call upon the name of the Lord" (Gen 4:26).

I also learned that true worship is transcendent, that is, it is bigger than me, or my local congregation. We are united to those most ancient of believers in the Lord, that "great . . . cloud of witnesses" (Heb 12:1), as we too assemble for worship, on the Lord's Day as the Lord's holy people. We too are enabled to serve God by worshipping him because he has first served us in lavishing abundant grace upon us in his Son, Jesus Christ (Eph 1:7–8), who was born, lived perfectly in our place, died in our place, and was "raised

---

1. For a classic Reformed understanding that public worship is the culmination of the Christian life, see Clarkson, "Public Worship," 3.187–209.

for our justification" (Rom 4:25). He continues to serve us by calling us to himself by the power of the Holy Spirit, speaking his precious promises to us in his Word, feeding us with spiritual food in the sacraments, and sending us into the world in his power and Spirit. In response to his amazing grace, we offer him thankful, heartfelt worship in the power of the Holy Spirit. Worship, then, is what we do in response to God serving us in grace.

In saying all of this by way of introduction, I recognize that the service in a *Reformed* church may be a different experience for you. Let me put you at ease by saying that it was not only different for me, but also for many of those in the church I founded (Oceanside United Reformed Church) as well as many who are coming to Reformed churches across the world out of other church backgrounds.

I also recognize that the service may seem "Catholic" to you. Again, let me assure you that we are not *Roman* Catholic. We are Christian and Protestant churches.[2] In the Protestant Reformation of the sixteenth century, men such as Martin Luther, Martin Bucer, and John Calvin sought to reform the existing Church and its public services according to Scripture while also being informed by the early Church. They took what existed and removed all the things that were not scriptural, nor ancient. Therefore, we do not have a priest, but a minister (servant) of the Word. He does not wear priestly vestments, but simple and dignified attire. We do not have an altar, but a communion table. We do not pray to Mary or the saints, but to the Father, through Jesus Christ, in the power of the Holy Spirit (Eph 2:18; 1 Peter 2:5). We do not pray for the dead, but for the living needs of the church and the world.

The purpose of this booklet, then, is to educate and acquaint you with the basics of our services as Reformed churches, so that you will know what to expect when among us. In knowing what to expect, we pray that you will more actively, joyfully, and meaningfully respond to all you hear and see with us: "Amen! Praise the Lord!" (Ps 106:48)

Venite exultemus Domino! Oh, come let us sing to the Lord!

2. For a basic introduction to the history and theology of a Reformed church, see Hyde, Welcome to a Reformed Church.

1

The Big Picture

As WE BEGIN, LET me first give you "the big picture" of our services. When you step into worship with us, there may seem to be a lot of pieces to what is happening that you are unable to put together. Just like you need the picture of a completed puzzle while putting the pieces together, so too I want to give you the big principles behind what we do when we assemble, and why we do them. This means this chapter is self-consciously theological in orientation. The reason for this is that liturgy reflects theology in every church regardless of how "liturgical" it is or how "free" it is. How we worship is a reflection of what we believe about God. In a word, our worship is our theology in practice. It is only after this that we will look at the specific things within the service of our Triune God of grace in our next two chapters.

A MEETING WITH GOD

When you gather with us, you can expect to meet with the Triune God who is "Holy, Holy, Holy" (Isa 6:3; Rev 4:8). Like Moses met with the Lord "face to face, as a man speaks to his friend" in the tent of meeting (Exod 33:7–11), so now all of God's people enter that presence "by the new and living way that [Jesus] opened for us through the curtain, that is, through his flesh" (Heb 10:20), to meet with God. This is the wonder of worship. The God of the universe has condescended ("stooped down") to us in his Son, Jesus Christ, and become our redeemer to draw into his presence by the power of the Holy Spirit. Because we meet with this great God, our services are joyful, reverent, and purposeful.

We believe the Bible is clear in teaching that our God is a sovereign, covenant-making God. He first created Adam and Eve in a covenant relationship with himself (Hos 6:7). He then came to the rescue after Adam severed that relationship by his sin. When the Lord God came to the rescue we call that "the covenant of grace." In Genesis 3:15 we hear of its beginning, as the Lord God promised that a seed would come from the woman to crush the head of the serpent's seed. This covenant of grace continued as the Lord gathered his people to meet with him in worship through history to the climax of redemption in Jesus Christ, the seed of the woman (Gal 4:4) who crushed Satan (John 12:31; Rev 12). Therefore, because of our sin and depravity, God always initiates worship because we never would apart from his Spirit calling us to do so. Our worship reflects these scriptural teachings of God's sovereignty and holiness, our horrible blindness in sin, and God's condescending to us in grace and mercy in his meeting with us.

A DIALOGUE

Since all biblical covenants have two sides, one, which speaks, and another, which responds, the meeting of worship is a dialog between our great God who speaks to us in grace while we respond to him in gratitude. This means that the structure and "feel" of Reformed worship is different than the typical worship of a modern evangelical church. So many modern churches reverse this order of *God's* call and then *our* response—grace then gratitude—and put the lengthy time of our singing first and then the message from the Word second. In fact, this contemporary pattern of an extended period of "worship," when the people sing, and the "message," when the pastor speaks, oftentimes leading to the "altar call" (a substitute for the sacrament of the Lord's Supper), comes from nineteenth

century American frontier revival meetings, and not Scripture. The theology behind this contemporary pattern of worship is to place the people's work in worship before God's work. The inevitable result is ads a works-oriented theology and piety, in which free will and obedience-based blessing is central.

Since our worship expresses our theology, the grace of God is in the primary place and our gratitude is in the secondary place. Therefore our services follow the biblical pattern in having a "call-response" structure, in which God speaks to us and we respond to him: "we assemble and meet together to render thanks for the great benefits that we have received at his hands, to set forth his most worthy praise, to hear his most holy Word, and to ask those things which are requisite and necessary, as well for the body as the soul" (BCP). In John's words, "We love because he first loved us" (1 John 4:19). Let me give an illustration of this in the chart below.

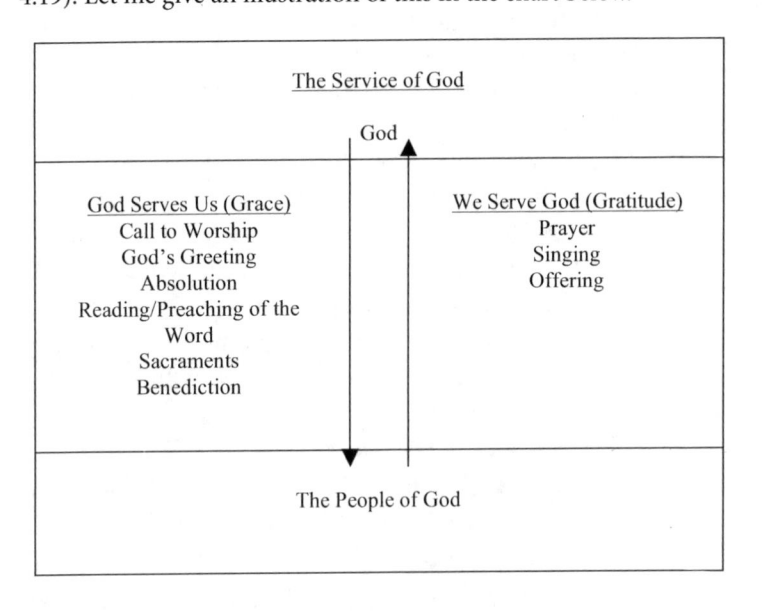

The Service of God

God

God Serves Us (Grace)
Call to Worship
God's Greeting
Absolution
Reading/Preaching of the Word
Sacraments
Benediction

We Serve God (Gratitude)
Prayer
Singing
Offering

The People of God

REVERENCE AND TRANSCENDENCE

The Scriptures teach us that God seeks a people to worship him in Spirit and in truth (John 4:24) and those who enter his presence, enter holy ground (Exod 3:5). This is why the people of God in Scripture are called to "offer to God acceptable worship, *with reverence and awe*, for our God is a consuming fire" (Heb 12:29; Deut 4:24) and to "rejoice *with trembling*" (Ps 2:11). The Bible teaches that the service of the Lord (remember, we call our meeting as a church a "service" because it is the Lord's service to us, and our service to him) is not about being entertained, having an emotional experience, or experimenting with the latest fads. It is about our Triune God who sits upon the heavenly throne, who gives his gifts to his people and who receives glory from them in return (Rev 4–5). Reformed worship lifts our hearts and minds from ourselves and onto the glory of God in Christ; off this world and onto the hope of "the life of the world to come" (*Nicene Creed*).

Since we worship in reverence our service is done "decently and in order" (1 Cor 14:40), as we utilize an order of service in historical continuity with ages of Christians past. Not only is this reformed according to Scripture, it is also informed according to the history of the Church. Reformed services follow the basic pattern of worship in early church descriptions such writings as The Didache (A.D. 120), Justin Martyr's First Apology (A.D. 155), and Tertullian's Apology (A.D. 197). These glimpses into the ancient church were the basis for the historic liturgies of the Protestant Reformation, such as the Strasbourg Liturgy (1539), from the influential city where Martin Bucer ministered; the Genevan Liturgy (1545), of John Calvin; the Book of Common Prayer (1552), written by Thomas Cranmer and revised by Martin Bucer, Peter Martyr Vermigli, and John Hooper for the English Reformation; and the Heidelberg Liturgy (1563), from the center of German Reformed theology. The Protestant Reformation, then, was just that: a reformation of what existed, not a restoration of what was lost. Our forefathers did not see themselves as "throwing the baby out with the bath water," but took what existed from medieval worship and went "back to the sources" (Latin, *ad fontes*) of Scripture and the

ancient church as a testimony of the truth of Scripture. The Reformers stripped the Medieval Mass of its idolatry and extra-scriptural content down to its biblical and ancient core; they did not re-invent the wheel.[1]

Therefore, what you experience as you gather with us is a fully biblical service in the same vein as the historic liturgies of the ancient Church, which the Protestant Reformers revived during the sixteenth century. Our hope is to communicate these eternal principles of God's Word, as passed down through the centuries, in a meaningful way to a twenty-first century world. It is not our desire to simply reproduce old tradition for the sake of being traditional, but we seek to be biblical and always reforming in the light of Scripture.

A COMMON SERVICE

When you join us, you can also expect to be a participant. Historic Christian and Protestant worship is "common worship." This means that the congregation is active, not passive. We express the love, praise, and adoration we each have in our hearts for God the Holy Trinity in a corporate way as we enter together into his presence to join in a dialog. Our service is a conversation between God and his people, in which he speaks and we respond. Therefore, we do not sit back and let a priest, "worship leader," or "praise band" do the work since the "liturgy" literally is "the work of the people."

Therefore, upon entering the place of worship, you will receive a bulletin that contains the order of service, or, "liturgy." Because the church in heaven worships with set forms and patterns, so do we (Rev 4–5). This allows us to sing corporately: "Come, let us worship and bow down; let us kneel before the Lord our God our Maker" (Ps 95:6). This allows us to pray corporately: "Our Father" (Matt 6:9). This allows us to confess corporately our faith in the Nicene Creed: "We believe in one God." Our response of worship, then, is with one voice and one heart.

---

1. For more on this see Hyde, "According to the Custom of the Ancient Church? Examining the Roots of John Calvin's Liturgy," 189–211.

You will notice that Scripture and scriptural language fills the entire service in every aspect, from our responses and songs, to our prayers and the reading of Scripture itself. The benefit of this is that we will learn "the word of Christ" and it will "dwell in [us] richly," whether we are young or old, a baptized child, a new convert, or an old saint. This enables us to respond with "thankfulness in [our] hearts" (Col 3:16).

CHILDREN IN THE SERVICE

Reformed services are not only common and corporate; they are also covenantal. Remember, worship reflects theology. As a Reformed church we believe that the Scriptures teach that the Church is a community of all in covenant with God, which means infants "as well as their parents, belong to the covenant and people of God" (HC, Q&A 74). It is on the basis of at least one parent that professes faith in Christ and obedience to him that their children "are in that respect within the covenant" (WLC, Q&A 166).[2] Corporate worship, then, is the place where we communally instruct our children in "the faith once for all delivered to the saints" (Jude 3). This means children are in our services. This is consistent with Israel's practice so many generations ago, as the psalmist records:

> We will not hide them [the works of the Lord]
>   from their children,
> but tell to the coming generation
> the glorious deeds of the LORD, and his might,
> and the wonders that he has done (Ps 78:4).

This means young and old, and all in between in the church, belong to the body of believers. This is one of the hardest things for new visitors and new members of our churches to adapt to as many are used to some form of "children's church." Yet, the Bible calls all God's people, young and old, to "make a joyful noise to the Lord" (Ps 100:1). Therefore the praise and noises of Jesus' little ones fills

---

2. For more on this, see Hyde, Jesus Loves the Little Children, 29–47.

our service. We accept this as members of the church because we are also members of each other (Rom 12:4–5; 1 Cor 12:12–27).

We understand this is a different way of worshipping and that it is difficult. For these reasons, most of our churches do provide a nursery or cry room for little children, to assist when needed. If you are not sure if your child is too old or you just do not know what to do, ask us; we are here to help. Finally, as you learn to appreciate this covenantal worship, with adults and children, you will also need to begin teaching your children about the service and how to participate. Some basic ways you can help your child before, during, and after the service are:

1. Singing a "Song of the Week" or "Song of the Month" during the week as well as reading the Scripture texts that will be read on Sunday before you come to the service with your children. If your church's liturgy is not posted on the church website or sent out via e-mail, just ask the pastor to help with this.

2. If you need a Bible or a copy of a hymnal, just ask and we will provide you with one.

3. Help your children participate by giving them a bulletin, hymnal, and/or Bible. You may also share one with them. Have them circle the words in the order of service that they hear during the sermon and even begin to write down some sermon notes.

4. Talk quietly to your children during the service about what is going on. Feel free to explain things to them and ask them questions. This helps them engage.

5. Another way to teach your children to participate is to teach them to give a part of the money they may have or allow them to give the family offering each week.

6. Talk to your children about the sermon and service on the way home, while it is fresh in their memories. Discuss it over lunch or before you pray at night.[3]

---

3. For an excellent resource on children in worship, see Castleman, *Parenting in the Pew*.

THE "LITURGY"

Our English word "liturgy" comes from an ancient Greek word for "service." From this word we get the idea that worship is service. As we said above, it is God's service to us, and our service to God. A liturgy is simply the order in which this service takes place. Every church, therefore, is liturgical. "Liturgy" is not something only some churches have, such as the Roman Catholic Church or "traditional" churches, but every church in the world has a liturgy. Whether or not a particular church has a more structured or informal service, or whether a "liturgy" is printed in the bulletin and followed or not, does not make some churches liturgical and some not. The question we must ask ourselves, is not whether a church has a liturgy, but since we have one, is it biblical? Therefore let us put it in the light of Scripture to see whether it is communicating the great truths about God, Christ, and us.

THE REGULATIVE PRINCIPLE

Finally, and most importantly in a Reformed church, we believe that we are not to worship God "in any other way than he has commanded in his Word" (HC, Q&A 96). This means we believe the particular things in the service of God are clearly commanded to us by God himself, set forth in biblical examples, or deduced by solid principles of interpretation from the inspired Word of God. It is only in this way that "we may serve God acceptably with reverence and godly fear" (Heb 12:28). We call this the "Regulative Principle." We see this taught in the Ten Commandments, for example, where the Lord, the one true God, commands his people to worship him alone (first Commandment) and that they are to do this in the way he says (second Commandment).

The Scriptures abound with God sufficiently explaining to his people how he serves us and how he desires and deserves us to serve him. The acceptable elements of the service of the Triune God, generally speaking, are elements of his service to us in the Word and Sacraments and our service to him in Prayer (Acts 2:42 cf. HC, Q&A 103).

God serves us when he speaks to us in his Word. In particular, this is expressed when he calls us to worship with his Word (Ps 95), greets us with his Word (Rev 1:4–5), speaks what he requires of us in his Word in the Law (Exod 20; Deut 5; Ezra 8:1–8), declares us forgiven in his Word (1 John 1:9; Matt 18:18; John 20:23), speaks in the reading of the Word that is to be proclaimed (1 Tim 4:13), speaks through the voice of his minister in the preaching of the Word (2 Tim 4:2), and send us out into the world with his grace in the benediction from the Word (Num 6:24–26; 2 Cor 13:14). The Lord also serves us in grace when the sacraments of Baptism and the Lord's Supper are done according to Christ's commands (Luke 22:17–20; 1 Cor 11:23–26). Following Augustine (354–430) we call these "visible" words, as they are meant to communicate to us tangibly what the promises of the Word communicate audibly.

In response, we serve God in prayer. Our prayers are expressed in various particular ways. The giving of offerings (1 Cor 16:2), in biblical terms, is the paying of a vow of thanks. Furthermore, there is a plethora of scriptural types of prayers. There is the pastoral prayer (1 Tim 2:1), confession of sins (Ps 51), adoration of God (Ps 8), and congregational singing, especially of the inspired songbook of the covenant people, the Psalter (Eph 5:19; Col 3:16). Reformed churches are Psalm-singing churches. While some sing these exclusively, at minimum the Psalms make up the principal part of our singing, while other songs that faithfully and fully reflect the teaching of Scripture may be sung as well.

This "big picture" of our public service, then, is intended to give you the reasons why we do what we do in our assemblies. We follow the biblical idea that the service is a meeting with our great and gracious God to engage in the dialog of grace and gratitude in a reverent and transcendent manner. This meeting involves all God's people, including children, as we together follow the biblical pattern in the way God commands in his Word.

2

The Center-Points of Our Service

HAVING EXAMINED THE "WHY" of our service, let us examine the "what" as well. In this chapter, we will reflect upon the central points of our services, which are the aforementioned Word, sacraments, and prayer. These especially have center stage since they are "the outward and ordinary means whereby Christ communicates to his church the benefits of his mediation" (WLC, Q&A 154).

THE MEANS OF GRACE

When you join us, you will notice that the primary focus is on what we call "the means of grace." The Scriptures teach us that the Holy Spirit uses various outward means (Latin, *media*) to create true faith in us, to confirm continually that faith, and to build up the community of believers.[1] For example, he used circumcision with Abraham (Gen 17), the Passover lamb with the Israelites in Egypt (Exod 12), and the tabernacle with Israel in the wilderness (Exod 25–40). Through means God offers and applies his grace to meet our true needs—forgiveness of our sins before us as well as empowerment to be reconciled with our neighbors—not what we perceive as our "felt needs" nor what the world tells us we need.

---

1. For more on this topic see Hyde, In Living Color.

There are many means, broadly speaking, that Christ uses to bless us with his grace throughout our lives. For example, he uses suffering in our lives, which conforms us to himself (1 Peter 4:12–16). There are also means, strictly speaking, that Christ uses to bless us with his grace in public assemblies—the reading of the Word of God (1 Tim 4:13), the preaching of the Word of God (2 Tim 4:1–5), the celebration of the Sacraments of baptism (Matt 28:18-20; Col 2:11–12) and the Lord's Supper (1 Cor 11:17–34), as well as prayer (1 Tim 2:1–3).

THE WORD

The Reading of the Word

As a Reformed church, we believe that reading the Bible together in public is essential. As one of our historic statements of faith says, "The Spirit of God maketh the reading, but especially the preaching of the word, an effectual means" (WLC, Q&A 155). While preaching is especially used by the Holy Spirit, the reading of the Word is used by him as well. This is based, for example, on Paul's exhortation to young pastor Timothy: "Until I come, devote yourself to the public reading of Scripture" (1 Tim 4:13). As a "part of the publick worship of God" reading the Word is "sanctified by him for the edifying of his people." This is why the *Westminster Directory for the Publick Worship of God* (1645) went on to say that "it is convenient, that ordinarily one chapter of each Testament be read at every meeting; and sometimes more, where the chapters be short, or the coherence of matter requireth it" and that "all the canonical books be read over in order, that the people may be better acquainted with the whole body of the scriptures." In fact, some Reformed churches set up a calendar of readings to be read every morning and every evening of the year in churches "that the people . . . might continually profit more and more in the knowledge of God, and be the more inflamed with the love of his true Religion" (*BCP*). Reformed worship, therefore, is to be Bible-saturated worship.

The Centrality of Preaching

The pure preaching of the Gospel is the first mark of a true church (BC, article 29). This means it is the most important thing we do. By means of the preaching of the "word of Christ" (Rom 10:17; 1:16; 1 Cor 1:21), the Holy Spirit creates true faith in our sinful hearts (HC, Q&A 65; BC, article 24) so that "men may be brought to believe" in Christ (CD, 1.3) and that the people of God may be built up in faith (Eph 4:11–16; 1 Tim 4:6; 2 Tim 2:2; 3:16–17). Without preaching there would be no salvation; there would be no church. Gospel preaching, then, is a "key of the kingdom of heaven," as it opens to sinners the door of salvation in Christ (HC, Q&A 83, 84)

Our Protestant forefathers understood the essential nature of preaching in the life of the Church, as it is the means of God bringing us the totality of our salvation—regeneration, justification, sanctification, and glorification. This understanding brought them into direct conflict with the leaders of their day in the Roman Catholic Church, who insisted on the "relevant" method of the day in instructing the people with images, as "books of the laity." Our forefathers rejected these "seeker-sensitive" methods, saying, ". . . we should not be wiser than God, who will not have his people taught by dumb idols, but by the lively preaching of his Word" (HC, Q&A 98).

Christ-Centered Preaching

Because preaching is the primary means of grace, biblical preaching focuses upon Jesus Christ and his work *for us* in his perfect life, sacrificial death, and glorious resurrection (2 Cor 4:5–7). Biblical preaching also focuses upon Jesus Christ and his work *in us* by the power of the Holy Spirit to renew our hearts. Biblical, Christ-centered preaching accomplishes this by properly distinguishing between the strict concepts of the Law and the Gospel—the bad news and the good news. Reformed preaching, then, is inherently evangelistic. In preaching the Law, we hear God's perfect demands, which we cannot meet, and thus our need for a Savior. In preaching the Gospel, we hear how Christ alone fulfills the Law's demands

and satisfies our deepest of needs as "the bread from heaven" (John 6:50). "What, therefore, neither the light of nature nor the law could do, that God performs by the operation of his Holy Spirit through the word or ministry of reconciliation: which is the glad tidings concerning the Messiah" (CD, 3/4.6).

Therefore, when God meets with us, he puts to death our old, sinful nature through the preaching of the strictness of the Law, and renews and revives our new man, by the preaching of the Gospel, thus enabling us to repent, to believe, and to love that same Law in its use as a guide for godliness.

Catechetical Preaching

One distinctive feature of the preaching ministry in Reformed churches is the time-honored tradition of "catechetical" preaching, that is, preaching through the cardinal doctrines and duties of the Christian religion, utilizing time-honored outlines such as the Apostles' Creed, Ten Commandments, and Lord's Prayer. Catechetical preaching was a hallmark of the ancient church, for example, in the preaching of Augustine and Cyril of Jerusalem. Our Reformation forefathers revived this practice. Catechetical preaching ensures that the pastor explains the basics of the Christian Faith to the congregation on a regular basis. This is why the *Heidelberg Catechism* and *Westminster Shorter Catechism* are so helpful in accomplishing this, as they explains the basics of Christian faith (Apostles' Creed and Sacraments), hope (Lord's Prayer), and love (Ten Commandments).

THE SACRAMENTS

In the joyful celebration of the holy sacraments, the Holy Spirit confirms and assures our faith in Jesus Christ (Rom 4:11). He does this by directing our faith to the one sacrifice of Jesus Christ on the cross as the only ground of our salvation (HC, Q&A 67). The sacraments are

> ... visible, holy signs and seals, appointed of God for this
> end, that by the use thereof he may the more fully declare
> and seal to us the promise of the Gospel; namely, that
> he grants us out of free grace the forgiveness of sins and
> everlasting life, for the sake of the one sacrifice of Christ
> accomplished on the cross (HC, Q&A 66).

These two tangible expressions of God's grace are the second
mark of a true church (BC, article 29).

Baptism

Baptism is the one-time act of initiation into the New Covenant
and Church of God, distinguishing its recipients from the rest of
the world (BC, article 34; *Thirty-Nine Articles*, article 27). For this
reason, it is administered in our churches only by ministers of the
Word in a public service. Baptism is a sign and seal (assurance) that
Christ's blood and Spirit washes us from our sins when we repent
and believe (HC, Q&A 69). Baptism, then, is the sign and seal that
Christ's blood washes away our sins and that his Spirit renews us so
we may die to sin and live to righteousness (HC, Q&A 70).

The Recipients of Baptism

As historic Christians, we follow the practice of the universal
Church in baptizing both adults who convert to the Christian Faith
and are afterwards instructed and examined concerning their doctrine and life before the ruling body of the church and the children
of professing believers (BC, article 34; HC, Q&A 74; *Thirty-Nine
Articles*, article 27).

We follow this historic practice of the Church in baptizing
our children because in the Old and New Testaments, the children
of believers are included in the visible covenant relationship with
the Lord, which we call the church (Gen 17:7; Exod 20:12; Matt
19:13–15; Acts 2:39; 1 Cor 7:14; Eph 6:1–3; Col 3:20). The sign of
belonging to the covenant people in the Old Testament was circumcision, which was administered to believing males, all males in their

household, whether children or servants, and to all who desired to become members of Israel (Gen 17:9–14). The sign of belonging to the covenant people in the New Testament is baptism, which Paul calls the Christians' circumcision (Col 2:11–12). This was, and continues to be, administered to believers, their households, and to all who are far off and come to faith in Jesus (Acts 2:39; 16:15, 16:31; 1 Cor 1:16).

The Lord's Supper

The sacrament of Holy Communion is the ongoing action of spiritual nourishment for the people of God, who are like the wilderness generation of Israel (1 Cor 10). This holy meal is a sign and seal that Christ's body and blood was shed for us on the cross and that Christ feeds and nourishes us to everlasting life with his body and blood (HC, Q&A 75; BC, article 35; John 6), which are the "true meat and drink of our souls" (HC, Q&A 79). To "eat" Christ's body and "drink" his blood means that we embrace his sufferings for our forgiveness and life and to become more and more united to him by the Holy Spirit, so that we become flesh of his flesh and bone of his bone (HC, Q&A 76).

As a Reformed church, we believe the Lord's Supper involves the "real presence" of Jesus Christ. This means that while it is more than a symbol the bread and wine do not become the body and blood of Christ (HC, Q&A 80). The Lord's Supper, ultimately, is a profound mystery in which the Holy Spirit ineffably lifts our hearts by faith to where Christ is, at the right hand of God, and feeds us there with Christ. Therefore, the Lord's Supper is better to experience than to understand; to apprehend not comprehend.

Those We Welcome at the Lord's Table

Since the Lord's Supper is a time of fellowship between Christ and his people, Reformed churches take seriously those who join in this sacred meal. If you do not trust in Jesus Christ alone for your salvation we welcome you to our service, but we must ask you to abstain

from the Lord's Table. The apostle Paul warns against unworthy eating, saying, "Whoever eats this bread or drinks this cup of the Lord in an unworthy manner will be guilty of the body and blood of the Lord" (1 Cor 11:27; HC, Q&A 82). If you are not a Christian, we pray that you will accept the good news of salvation in Jesus Christ by turning from yourself and casting yourself before Jesus Christ, trusting in his perfect life, sacrificial death, and glorious resurrection. If this describes you, please speak with the Pastor after the service.

We do not do this to judge or look down upon people, but because we believe Christ has given the task of supervising participation at the Lord's Table to elders of local churches. We welcome all to our services and pray that all will come to believe in Christ and unite themselves to Christ's people in the church. We want to make sure all who partake are believers in Christ and in a right relationship with his church. Every church is going to have its own particular criteria, but generally speaking, the elders are looking for those who desire to eat and drink with us to be members of a biblical church and to be living in a godly manner. Please speak with a pastor and/or elder about joining us at the Table.

What About Children?

You may be thinking that since we baptize children of believers that this means we also welcome our children to partake of the Lord's Supper. This is not the case. The reason for our practice is that we believe the Scriptures require that the Lord's Supper be administered only to those who have publicly professed their faith in the presence of God and his holy church (1 Cor 11:24–25, 28).

This means that children who have yet to be examined by their elders and who have yet to make a public profession of faith in Jesus Christ before the congregation are to abstain from the Lord's Supper. We do want to make clear, though, that we desire all of our children to make a public profession of faith in Jesus Christ and to join us at the Lord's Table.

PRAYER

Finally, prayer is the third center point of our public services. While the Word and sacraments are most strictly the means of grace we refer to in Reformed terminology, since they are spoken and given to us from a minister as a representative of Christ, prayer is also a means. Prayer is a balance between our response to God's grace and a means of receiving his grace:

> Q. Why is prayer necessary for Christians?
>
> A. Because it is the chief part of the thankfulness which God requires of us, and because God will give his grace and Holy Spirit only to such as earnestly and without ceasing beg them from him and render thanks unto him for them. (HC, Q&A 116)

Jesus spoke this way when he said the children of God are to ask, seek, and knock for God's good gifts (Matt 7:7–11), and in particular his greatest gift to us, the Holy Spirit (Luke 11:13). The book of Hebrews exhorts us on the basis of Jesus' high priestly ministry "with confidence draw near to the throne of grace." Why? "That we may receive mercy and find grace to help in time of need" (Heb. 4:16). Our services, then, are full of prayer. We approach God in adoration. We acknowledge and confess our sins. We pray for the Holy Spirit's blessing upon the reading and preaching of the Word. We lift our hearts in intercession for the needs of the world and the church. We give thanks before and after the celebration of the sacraments.

As the center-points of our service, the reading and preaching of the Word of God and the celebration of the two sacraments are God's gracious service to us. By these means he offers his grace, saying, "taste and see that the Lord is good" (Ps 34:8). And as we receive his gracious offer we respond to him in grateful prayer from the bottom of our hearts.

3

A Walk through a Sample Morning & Evening Service

How DO THE BASIC big picture principles and the primacy of the means of grace in the foregoing come together in a typical service in a Reformed church? That is what we will explore in this chapter, by walking you through a sample morning and evening service that the congregation I serve uses and pointing out how everything flows together.[1] As this walk-through will show, Reformed liturgy focuses upon communicating and communing. Jesus communicates his grace to us and we communicate back to him; he communes with us in grace and we commune with him in gratitude. Keep in mind that while there is liturgical variation from church to church, and from week to week within any local church, the elements and basic pattern below will be the same.

OUTLINED MORNING SERVICE

Entering the Presence of God

    Call to Worship

    God's Greeting

    Prayer

1. For weekly bulletins with liturgies, see www.oceansideurc.org.

Confession & Forgiveness

    Reading of the Law

    Prayer of Confession

    Declaration of Forgiveness/Absolution

Praise of God

    Scripture Responses

    Song

    Creed

    Pastoral Prayer

    Offering

The Word of God

    Prayer for Illumination

    Scripture Reading

    Sermon

Holy Communion

    Song

    Exhortation

    Comforting Words

    Sursum Corda

    Prayer

    Words of Institution

    Delivery

    Prayer of Thanksgiving

    Song

Sending Into the World

Benediction

EXPLAINING THE MORNING SERVICE

Entering the Presence of God

Call to Worship

As we transition from the world to worship, whether with some musical prelude or a time of silence, we acknowledge that we are entering the presence of *God* in worship, recognizing that the place we stand is "holy ground" (Exod 3:5).

The first words we hear are those of our Lord himself. In some churches the words of Matthew 28:19 are declared: "In the name of the Father, and of the Son, and of the Holy Spirit." We heard these words for the first time at our baptism. Now, they call us back to the fact that we are citizens of the kingdom of God. In the call to worship the minister reads from the Word of God, calling us out of the world to enter God's heavenly presence before his throne of grace in order to offer him praise and adoration: "Come, let us worship and bow down" (Ps 95:1–7); "Let us draw near" (Heb 10:19–22); "Worthy are you, our Lord and God, to receive glory and honor and power" (Rev 4:11).

God's Greeting

Now that the King of heaven has summoned us to stand before him at his call, he graciously welcomes us into his presence. The minister uses words such as Revelation 1:4–5, as each Person of the Trinity give us their "grace and peace."

Prayer

Our response to this is one of adoration and praise in prayer, whether by the minister or corporately by the congregation. Here are two examples of a prayer of invocation, that is, a prayer that calls upon God to be present:

> Almighty God, to you our hearts are open, our desires are known, and from you no secrets are hid: cleanse the thoughts of our hearts by the gracious power of your Holy Spirit, that we may perfectly love you and worthily magnify your holy name; through Christ our Lord. Amen. (Adapted from the BCP)

> Almighty and everlasting God, you are always more ready to hear than we are to pray, and to give more than we desire, or deserve; pour down upon us the abundance of your mercy; forgiving us those things of which our conscience is afraid, and giving us those good things which we are not worthy to ask, except through the merits and mediation of Jesus Christ, your Son, our Lord. Amen. (Adapted from the BCP)

Confession & Forgiveness

Reading of the Law

Having entered God presence and approached his throne of grace in reverence and joy, God speaks to us his Law. This can be done by the minister reading the Ten Commandments (Exod 20:1–17) or by doing so responsively with the congregation. Jesus' summary of the Law (Matt 22:34–40) or any other biblical text that lays out God's will for our lives may also be used. In the reading of the Law, we hear God's perfect and righteous demands for us to stand before him. Since God is perfect and we are sinful, the Law teaches us "that all our life long we live we may learn more and more to know our sinful nature, and so become more earnest in seeking remission of sins and righteousness in Christ." In the law we also hear how we

as the redeemed people of the Lord are to live: "that we may continually strive and beg from God the grace of the Holy Ghost, so as to become more and more changed into the image of God, till we attain finally to full perfection after this life" (HC, Q&A 115).

Prayer of Confession

Recognizing just how much we have failed to live up to God's standards and do not deserve to stand before the holy God of the universe, we pause to confess our sins. We do this in the knowledge that "the sacrifices of God are a broken spirit; a broken and contrite heart," which he "will not despise" (Ps 51:17). Since God speaks to the congregation in the Law, it is fitting for the congregation to pray corporately in confession, whether by singing or saying Psalm 51, or a prayer such as the following:

> Almighty and most merciful Father, we have erred, and strayed from your ways like lost sheep: we have followed too much the devices and desires of our own hearts. We have offended against your holy laws: we have left undone those things which we ought to have done; and we have done those things which we ought not to have done; and there is no health in us. But you, O Lord, have mercy upon us, miserable offenders. Spare those, O God, who confess their faults: restore those who are penitent; according to your promises declared unto mankind in Christ Jesus our Lord. And grant, O most merciful Father, for his sake; that we may hereafter live a godly, righteous, and sober life, to the glory of your holy Name. Amen. (Adapted from the BCP)

> Our Father, we are sinful and You are holy. We recognize that we have heard in Your Law difficult words knowing how often we have offended You in thought, word, and deed, not only by obvious violations, but by failing to conform to its perfect commands, by what we have done and by what we have left undone. There is nothing in us that gives us reason for hope, for where we thought we were well, we are sick in soul. Where we thought we were holy, we are in truth unholy and ungrateful. Our

hearts are filled with the love of the world; our minds are dark and are assailed by doubts; our wills are too often given to selfishness and our bodies to laziness and unrighteousness. By sinning against our neighbors, we have also sinned against You, in Whose image they were created. Lord have mercy on us; Christ have mercy on us; Lord have mercy on us.[2]

Our time of confession concludes as we ask the Lord for the grace of his Holy Spirit to renew our hearts, singing David's words from Psalm 51:10–12, "Create in me a clean heart, O God."[3] For although "even the holiest men, while in this life, have only a small beginning of this obedience," by the power of the Spirit "with earnest purpose they begin to live, not only according to some, but according to all the commandments of God" (HC, Q&A 114).

Declaration of Forgiveness/Absolution

God speaks again to us in the declaration of forgiveness, also called the absolution. Having heard the Law, we now hear the promise of the Gospel. In God's Word, we learn that God has given his appointed ministers the authority to declare to the contrite and penitent that God forgives them for the sake of Christ (Matt 18:18; John 20:23). The absolution does not only declare that God's Law has been satisfied by the life, death, resurrection, and ascension of Christ, but that because of this work of Christ, *our* sins are forgiven and *we* are no longer under the condemnation of God's Law. The absolution is not a prayer, then, but a declaration from God to those who believe.[4]

2. This contemporary prayer was originally written by Dr. Michael Horton and is used by many United Reformed congregations.

3. The words and music to this song may be found in Sing! a new creation, #49.

4. For an historical survey of the absolution and a contemporary defense of its use, see Hyde, "Lost Keys: The Absolution in Reformed Liturgy," 140–66.

Praise of God

Scripture Responses

In response to the gift of God's forgiveness, the minister and con-gregation may recite responsively several texts of Scripture. When the minister says, "O LORD, open my lips," we exclaim, "And my mouth shall show forth your praise!" (Ps 51:15) In these words we pray that God, who has just cleansed us from sin, would enabled us by his Spirit to praise him rightly. They are an acknowledgement that we rely upon the sovereign work of the Holy Spirit to offer up worship to God. Again, grace is primary. The minister then says, "Praise the Lord!" With one voice, we cry out, "The Lord's name be praised!" (Ps 135:1) This is precisely what we go on to do in song, confession of faith, prayer, and offering.

Song

We believe it is important to sing often as a response to God's speak-ing to us. Our opening song is a "song of the month" that we sing in order to learn to praise God with biblical truth. This song is specifi-cally oriented towards praising God for his wonderful attributes of grace, holiness, and sovereignty, for example. We also sing various Psalms, hymns, and spiritual songs throughout the service. Often these have some relationship to an aspect of what God will say to us in the reading and preaching of his Word.

Creed

We confess our common faith with the *Apostles,' Nicene*, and *Atha-nasian Creeds*, which the early Church formulated as a way of unit-ing all Christians in a common Faith against the enemies of the Faith. When we make confession of our Faith in connection with the absolution, we declare who we are as the forgiven people of God. When this confession of the Faith is done prior to the Lord's Supper, it is a way of manifesting our unity in the Lord: "Because

there is one bread, we who are many are body, for we all partake of the one bread" (1 Cor 10:17).

As an aside, please note that when we confess the words "a holy catholic church" (Apostles' Creed) or "one holy, catholic and apostolic church" (Nicene Creed), we are confessing that we belong with all who have believed and will believe the gospel in all times and places. This is not a confession of the Roman Catholic Church but of the true catholic ("universal") Church. As well, the words "he descended into hell" (Apostles' Creed) speak of Christ's suffering hell for us throughout his whole life and especially on the cross (HC, Q&A 44).[5]

Pastoral Prayer

Having praised the Lord's name in song and confession of faith, we beseech his name in prayer for the needs of the Church and the world. The minister offers as the mouthpiece of the people the "prayers of the people." This pastoral prayer brings all our requests to God as a congregation. We pray for the civil government (1 Tim 2:1–2), the ministry (Matt 9:36–38), the salvation of all men (1 Tim 2:1, 3–4), the sanctification of the saints (Eph 6:18; Phil 1:9–11; Col 1:9–12), and for the afflicted (2 Cor 1:3-4; Jas 5:13–18), concluding with the Lord's Prayer, which is a basic biblical summary of all our petitions.

Offering

We also respond to God's forgiveness in a tangible way with our giving. This is an acknowledgement that God is our Provider and that our ability to create wealth comes only from him as we worship him by bringing the first of our increase to him.

---

5. For an explanation of this phrase, see Hyde, In Defense of the Descent.

The Word of God

Prayer for Illumination

The service moves from entering the presence of God, confession of sins, and praising the Lord, to hearing the voice of Jesus himself in the Word of God. To do this profitably, we begin by recognizing that we need the Holy Spirit to help us understand and apply God's truth in our lives. The prayer for illumination is a prayer for the work of the Holy Spirit to open our eyes, soften our hearts, and incline our wills to his will:

> O heavenly Father, your Word is perfect, restoring the soul, making wise the simple, and enlightening the eyes of the blind, and the power of God unto salvation for everyone that believes. We, however, are by nature blind and incapable of doing anything good, and you will comfort only those who have a broken and contrite heart and who revere your Word. We beseech you, therefore, to illumine our darkened minds with your Holy Spirit and give us a humble heart, free from all haughtiness and carnal wisdom, in order that we, hearing your Word, may rightly understand it and may regulate our lives accordingly. Will you also graciously convert those who are straying from the truth that we all in unity may serve you in true holiness and righteousness all the days of our life. These things we ask of you only for the sake of Christ, who promised to hear us. Amen.[6]

> Blessed Lord, who has caused all holy Scriptures to be written for our learning; grant that we may in such a way hear them, read, mark, learn, and inwardly digest them, that by patience and comfort of your holy Word, we may embrace, and ever hold fast the blessed hope of everlasting life, which you have given us in our Savior Jesus Christ. Amen. (Adapted from the BCP)

6. Psalter Hymnal, 185.

Scripture Reading

When the Word is opened and read, we hear Christ speaking from the top of the heavenly mountain to us his congregation below (Heb 12:18–29). Ordinarily, there is a reading from the Old Testament as well as the New Testament, since the Church is "built on the foundation of the apostles and prophets" (Eph 2:20). This ancient practice of several Scripture readings comes from the Jewish synagogue, in which there were readings from the Law (Genesis–Deuteronomy) and the Prophets (Joshua–Kings, Isaiah–Malachi), as well as the ancient practice of the Christian Church. What it shows us it that there is a unity in God's redemptive work, as we hear the Old Testament promises of a Savior and the New Testament fulfillments in Christ.

Sermon

As we have already seen, God has chosen to work in the lives of his people by using his written and preached Word. Preaching was the primary activity of Jesus and the apostles. The Scripture says preaching is a "foolish" means to convince and convert people, but that God has chosen this "weak" means to ensure that we give him credit for changing lives rather than crediting the eloquence or creativity of a minister (1 Cor 1:18–2:5). In the sermon we hear the living and active voice of our Lord Jesus Christ in the power of the Holy Spirit. This is why Paul called preaching not the word of man "but what it really is, the word of God" (1 Thess 2:13) and the Protestant Reformers said, "The preaching of the Word of God is the Word of God" (*Second Helvetic Confession*, 1.4).

Holy Communion

Song

The preached Word leads us into the visible Word, as we celebrate Holy Communion. As we move into this time of fellowship with our risen Savior, we respond to God's read and preached Word with a song that sets the theme of God's goodness and grace before us.

Exhortation

As said already, since communion is a holy meal and therefore a time of fellowship between Jesus Christ and his Church, the pastor "fences" the Table on behalf of all the pastors and elders who rule and oversee the church, warning all those who do not believe in Christ as well as those who have not united themselves to his visible Body, the Church, to abstain.

This is also a time of preparation for those who will partake of the bread and wine. The apostle Paul exhorts us diligently to "examine" ourselves before we "eat of the bread and drink of the cup" (1 Cor 11:28). Since the benefit of spiritually eating his flesh and drinking his blood is great so is the danger great if we receive it "in an unworthy manner" (1 Cor 11:27).

In the Lord's Supper, Christ's sheep hear the voice of their shepherd saying, "Taste and see that the Lord is good" (Ps 34:8). The minister, then, also issues an invitation to penitent and believing sinners, for example, with this beautiful tapestry of biblical language:

> This solemn warning is not designed, however, to discourage penitent sinners from coming to the holy sacrament. We do not come to the supper as though we were righteous in ourselves, but rather to testify that we are sinners and that we look to Jesus Christ for our salvation. Although we do not have perfect faith and do not serve and love God with all our hearts, and though we do not love our neighbors as we ought, we are confident that the Savior accepts us at His table when we come in humble faith, with sorrow for our sins, and with a will to follow Him as He commands.[7]

Comforting Words

The minister then reads several texts of Scripture that focus our hearts and minds upon the spiritual significance of the Lord's

7. "Celebration of the Lord's Supper: Form Number 3" in PH, 155–56.

Supper—feeding upon Christ and all his benefits for the nourishment of our souls. For example:

> Come to me, all who labor and are heavy laden, and I will give you rest. (Matt 11:28).

> For God so loved the world, that he gave his only Son, that whoever believes in him should not perish but have eternal life. (John 3:16)

> The saying is trustworthy and deserving of full acceptance, that Christ Jesus came into the world to save sinners, of whom I am the foremost. (1 Tim 1:15)

> If anyone does sin, we have an advocate with the Father, Jesus Christ the righteous. He is the propitiation for our sins. (1 John 2:1–2)

Sursum Corda

As a response to the Word and as a preface to prayer, we utilize the ancient response known as the *sursum corda* (Latin for "lift up your hearts"). These words come from the second century and express the heavenliness of communion, since we must enter heaven by faith to feed upon Christ. That we may be nourished with Christ, the true bread of heaven:

> Lift up your hearts.
> We lift them up to the Lord.[8]

Prayer

After our great Shepherd invites us his sheep to eat and drink in green pastures and besides still waters (Ps 23:2), we humbly approach the table he spreads before us (Ps 23:5) with a "Prayer of Humble Approach" such as the following:

---

8. For an explanation of the sursum corda, see Daniel R. Hyde, "Lift Up Your Hearts."

Almighty and everlasting God, who by the blood of your only begotten Son has secured for us a new and living way into the Holy of Holies, cleanse our minds and hearts by your Word and Spirit that we, your redeemed people, drawing close to you through this holy sacrament, may enjoy fellowship with the Holy Trinity through the body and blood of Christ our Savior. We know that our Ascended Savior does not live in temples made by hands, but is in heaven where he continues to intercede on our behalf. Through this sacrament, by Your own Word and Spirit, may these common elements be now set apart from ordinary use consecrated by You, so that just as truly as we eat and drink these elements by which our life is sustained, so truly we receive into our souls, for our spiritual life, the true body and true blood of Christ. We receive these by faith, which is the hand and mouth of our souls. Amen.[9]

We do not presume to come to this your table, O merciful Lord, trusting in our own righteousness, but in your great mercies. We are not worthy so much as to gather up the crumbs under your table. But you are our merciful and gracious Lord. Grant us, therefore, so to commemorate and celebrate in this breaking of bread the death of your dear Son Jesus Christ, that we may feed on him in our hearts by faith, and that we may be united to him, and he to us; who with you and the Holy Spirit is worthy of eternal thanks and praise. Amen. (Adapted from the BCP)

Words of Institution

Our hearts are then directed to the "Words of Institution" (1 Cor 11:23–26). In them we hear the sacramental words of Jesus, "This is my body which is for you . . . this cup is the new covenant in blood." God also calls us to participate actively and believingly in these promises in the words "do this in remembrance of me." Finally, as we participate in this feast, we join in a universal practice through

9. This contemporary prayer was originally written by Dr. Michael Horton and is used by many United Reformed congregations.

the ages, since Paul says, "For I received from the Lord what I also delivered to you."

Delivery

The manner in which we partake of the Lord's Supper, whether sitting, standing, or kneeling, is indifferent. The congregation that I serve is invited to get up out of their seats and to come forward to the table. Because in the Lord's Supper we come to Christ, we believe coming forward is a significant expression of this truth. Jesus "took bread, and after blessing it broke it *and gave it to the disciples*" and he "took a cup, and when he had given thanks *he gave it to them*" (Matt 26:26–27). So too Christ feeds and nourishes us "as certainly as [we] receive *from the hand of the minister*" (HC, Q&A 75) the bread and wine. In the preached Word, Christ promises us that our souls are in his hand, but how much more so in the visible Word, with his minister actually standing before us.

After all receive the bread and wine (the center ring contains grape juice), we sit and partake together in a foretaste of the great wedding feast of the lamb in heaven (Rev 19:6–10). As we partake of the bread, we hear the profound words: "The body of Christ, which was broken for you; preserve your body and soul unto everlasting life. Take and eat this in remembrance that Christ died for you, and feed on him in your heart by faith with thanksgiving." As we partake of the wine we hear: "The blood of Christ, which was shed for you: preserve your body and soul unto everlasting life. Drink this in remembrance that Christ's blood was shed for you, and be thankful."

Prayer of Thanksgiving

After recalling the wonderful grace of his Lord, David prayed, "What shall I render to the LORD?" (Ps 116:12a) In response to this question, he offered up prayer and praise to the Lord. We do the same, with a brief prayer of thanksgiving "for all his benefits to me" (Ps 116:12b).

Song

We then stand in response to the Lord's nourishing our souls at his table. In doing this we jointly praise his holy name with thanksgiving in songs that expresses gratitude for the spiritual blessings we have received in Christ. Particularly beloved psalms we use are Psalm 23, "The Lord's My Shepherd," Psalm 34, "The Lord I Will at All Times Bless," Psalm 103, "O Come, My Soul, Bless Thou the Lord," and Psalm 107, "O Praise the Lord, for He Is Good."[10]

Sending Into the World

Benediction

God has the final word of the service. He sends us out in joy to be led forth in his peace (Isa 55:12) to be the salt of the earth and the light of the world (Matt 5:13–16), as we hear words such as those spoken first by Aaron to the people of Israel: "The LORD bless you and keep you; the LORD make his face to shine upon you and be gracious to you; the LORD lift up his countenance upon you and give you peace" (Num 6:24–26).

OUTLINED EVENING SERVICE

Entering the Presence of God

> Call to Worship
>
> The Lord's Prayer
>
> Scripture Responses

Singing the Psalms

The Word of God

> Old & New Testament Reading

10. These songs can all be found in the Psalter Hymnal.

Sermon Text Reading

Sermon

Prayers

Prayer of Intercession

Prayer of Thanksgiving

Offering

Evening Song

Sending Into the World

Benediction

EXPLAINING THE EVENING SERVICE

I will speak more about the reasons for an evening service in the next chapter. For now, it is important to understand that the weekly pattern of a day of rest and worship in which the people of God assemble in the morning and in the evening is a tremendous blessing. Not only is it another opportunity to minister one to another, but it is especially another opportunity to hear God speak in his Word and to offer him praise and prayer. These two—Word and prayer—form the heart of the service. Whereas the morning service in my congregation lasts between an hour-and-fifteen minutes to an hour-and-a-half, the evening service lasts an hour. What follows is an adapted and shortened form of the *Book of Common Prayer's* service of evening prayer.

Entering the Presence of God

Call to Worship

Like the morning service, the evening begins with God's Word spoken to us, calling us to approach him in worship. One way to add variation to this is by using thematic calls to worship in the evening. For example, the following list of Scriptures expresses our thirst for God in worship:

> As a deer pants for flowing streams, so pants my soul for you, O God. My soul thirsts for God, for the living God. When shall I come and appear before God? (Ps 42:1–2)

> My soul yearns for you in the night; my spirit within me earnestly seeks you. (Isa 26:9)

> O God, you are my God; earnestly I seek you; my soul thirsts for you; my flesh faints for you, as in a dry and weary land where there is no water. (Ps 63:1)

> I stretch out my hands to you; my soul thirsts for you like a parched land. (Ps 143:6)

> If anyone thirsts, let him come to me and drink. (John 7:37)

The Lord's Prayer

Having been summoned, we offer supplication, utilizing the Lord's Prayer as a summary of all our "supplications, prayers, intercessions, and thanksgivings" (1 Tim 2:1) that are "necessary for soul and body" (HC, Q&A 118). Not only is the Lord's Prayer a pattern of praying "but [it] may also be used as a prayer, so that it be done with understanding, faith, reverence, and other graces necessary to the right performance of the duty of prayer" (WLC Q&A 187).

Scripture Responses

In this same spirit we then prayer responsively, as we did in the morning. The minister prays, "O Lord, open my lips," and the congregation prays, "And my mouth shall show forth your praise" (Ps 51:15), as we call upon God himself to enable us by the Holy Spirit to praise him rightly. We then cry out to God to come to our aid by his grace: "Make haste, O God, to deliver me. O Lord, make haste to help me" (Ps 70:1). Finally, as we prayed in the morning, we pray again: "Praise the Lord; the Lord's name be praised" (Ps 135:1).

Singing the Psalms

In the evening service we sing through the Psalms of the Old Testament in order, week by week, year after year. They are his Word; they are his helps to us in all the ups and downs of the Christian experience. At the conclusion we acknowledge that in the Psalms we sing of our Triune God. According to the custom of the ancient church, then, we sing the *Gloria Patri*:

> Glory be to the Father and to the Son
> and to the Holy Ghost;
> As it was in the beginning, is now and ever shall be,
> world without end.
> Amen. Amen.[11]

The Word of God

Old & New Testament Reading

At this point in our evening service we spend time meditating upon the Word. As was mentioned in chapter 2 above, we believe the reading of the Word of God is an act of worship. We take time to read a portion of the Old Testament and then a portion of the New Testament, as a way of hearing the Lord's story.

11. Psalter Hymnal, #492.

Sermon Text Reading

After this systematic reading of Scripture, another passage is read, which forms the text of the evening's sermon.

Sermon

Once again the read Word is preached. In the evening service it is customary to preach through the fundamental points of Christian doctrine and Christian living, as was mentioned in chapter 2.

Prayers

God's speech to us in his Word leads us to speak to him in prayer. In the evening service we spend significant time in prayer, both in intercession and thanksgiving.

Prayer of Intercession

For our time of intercession, we often begin with the ancient responses known as the *kyrie eleison*, "Lord have mercy." The minister prays, "Lord, have mercy upon us," we all pray, "Christ, have mercy upon us," and the minister again concludes, "Lord, have mercy upon us." These prayers express our humble approach to the throne of grace through Christ alone as well as stir us up to pray more.

We also often use a series of responsive prayers that express the basic prayers commanded in the Word of God. We pray for the merciful salvation of the Lord to be known by us: "O Lord, show your mercy upon us; and grant us your salvation." We pray for our nation: "O Lord, save the Republic; and mercifully hear us when we call upon you." We pray for the ministers of the gospel and those who hear them: "Endue your ministers with righteousness; and make your chosen people joyful." We pray for the gathering of the elect scattered among all people and all lands: "O Lord, save your people; and bless your inheritance." We pray for the welfare of the world: "Give peace in our time, O Lord; because there is none other

that fights for us, but only you, O God." We pray for our sanctification: "O God, make clean our hearts within us; and take not your Holy Spirit from us."

The majority of our time of intercession is then spent especially for the mission of the church locally and across the world, for our growth in godliness, for effectiveness in our evangelism and witnessing, and for the needs of the body of believers assembled before the face of God.

Prayer of Thanksgiving

We also lift up a prayer of thanksgiving with one voice with a beautiful expression of our heartfelt gratitude for all God has given us:

> Almighty God, Father of all mercies, we, your unworthy servants, do give you most humble and hearty thanks for all your goodness and loving-kindness to us, and to all men. We bless you for our creation, preservation, and all the blessings of this life; but above all, for your inestimable love in the redemption of the world by our Lord Jesus Christ; for the means of grace, and for the hope of glory. And, we beseech you, give us that due sense of all your mercies, that our hearts may be sincerely thankful; and that we may show forth your praise, not only with our lips, but in our lives, by giving up our selves to your service, and by walking before you in holiness and righteousness all our days; through Jesus Christ our Lord, to whom, with you and the Holy Spirit, be all honor and glory, world without end. Amen. (Adapted from the BCP)

Offering

Another Lord's Day offering is taken as a tangible expression of our grateful prayer to the Lord for his amazing grace to us in Jesus Christ.

Evening Song

Our time of prayer is concluded with a song that expresses the blessings of the day. One fitting song is "All Praise to Thee, My God This Night."[12]

> All praise to thee, my God, this night,
> For all the blessings of the light:
> Keep me, O keep me, King of kings,
> Beneath thine own almighty wings.
>
> Forgive me, Lord, for thy dear Son,
> The ill that I this day have done;
> That with the world, myself, and thee,
> I, ere I sleep, at peace may be.
>
> O may my soul on thee repose,
> And with sweet sleep mine eyelids close;
> Sleep that shall me more vigorous make
> To serve my God when I awake.
>
> Praise God, from whom all blessings flow;
> praise him, all creatures here below;
> praise him above, ye heavenly host:
> praise Father, Son, and Holy Ghost.

Sending Into the World

Benediction

We conclude our evening service, as in the morning, with God's very own word of grace, as he sends out into the world, saying, "May the God of hope fill you with all joy and peace in believing, so that by the power of the Holy Spirit you may abound in hope" (Rom 15:13).

---

12. Found in Trinity Hymnal, #401.

4

When Do We Meet for Service?

I HAVE EXPLAINED TO you the "why" of our service as well as the "what" of our service in the preceding chapters. I now need to answer the question of "when." I do not want to assume you understand why we meet on Sunday for the Lord's service to us and ours to him, so let me answer the question, "When do we meet for service?"

THE LORD'S DAY

In an age of the microwave mentality, of the sound byte, of the headline news, and of the craziness of a consumer society, we gather on Sunday, which the New Testament calls the Lord's Day (Rev 1:10). We do this to set aside our six days of labor, worry, and anxiety, in order to participate in something that is larger than us, that has been around longer than us, and that fills our hearts with true fulfillment.

From creation onward, the people of God worshipped on the seventh day, that is, Saturday. This day of rest every week was a "creation ordinance" that the Creator himself established by his example for his creatures to follow. Just as God ruled over creation and called his image-bearers to rule and exercise dominion over creation (Gen 1:26–28), and just as God worked six days and called

his image-bearers to work (Gen 2:15), so too God rested on the seventh day (Gen 2:2; Exod 20:11) and was refreshed (Exod 31:17), calling his image-bearers to rest as well. He signified this placing his benediction on that day as a set apart day when he "made it holy" (Gen 2:3). Of course, God's speaking of himself as "working" and "resting" is language that we understand so that God could give us a pattern to follow, while his being "refreshed" was his joy and satisfaction in all he had made. In the words of the psalmist, "May the Lord rejoice in his works" (Ps 104:31).

After the Lord's mighty deed of bringing his people out of Egypt and through the Red Sea, the Sabbath day took on even more significance as a covenant sign that the Lord sanctified his people (Exod 31:13). What did the sign signify? On that day the saints celebrated the reality that God created them (Exod 20:8–11) and redeemed them (Deut 5:12–15). Moreover, once a year the Day of Atonement fell on a Sabbath (Lev 16:30–31), and so the Sabbath also celebrated the Lord's forgiveness of his people.

Yet under the "old covenant" (Heb 8:6, 7, 13), that is, the administration of the covenant of grace with Israel from Moses (Exod 19) until Christ, the Sabbath day was extremely strict. In contrast to the administration with Abraham, God added the law to the administration of the covenant of grace under Moses (Lev 18:5; Gal 3:10, 19, 24). As with Adam, so Israel's work and rest spoke of eternal spiritual realities of obedience and eternal rest. Not only was no work to be done by the Israelites and their children, they were also to give rest to all in their household—servants, livestock, even sojourners (Exod 20:10). The Lord even gave regulatory laws over what could and could not be done. For example, if one even went out to gather sticks (Num. 15:32–36) in order to kindle a fire (Exod 35:1–3), he was to be put to death (Exod 31:14–15, 35:2). All this strictness was a part of the tutelage of the law, which was meant to lead Israel by the hand to Jesus Christ (Gal 3:24), who is the final sacrifice ending the old covenant (Heb 7:11–12, 18-19; 8:7, 13).

When Jesus rose from the dead on the first day of the week things changed. Christ, the Second Adam (1 Cor 15:45–47), finished the work that the first Adam failed to do (John 19:30; Rom 5:12–19). Therefore as Christians we are under the New Covenant

and our day of worship and celebration for the Lord's grace in Jesus Christ is the first day of the week, Sunday. On this day we commemorate and participate in the glorious reality that we have already entered God's eternal rest (Matt 11:28; Heb 4:10) and that we await the experience of the fullness of this rest in eternity in the new heavens and new earth (Rev 21–22).

Contrary to popular belief, we do not worship on Sunday because the early church fell away from the Bible and took over the pagan Roman *dies Solis* ("Sun-day") under Constantine. While the creation principle was that one day in seven was to be set aside for worship, the circumstances in which that principle is applied changed:

> ... from the beginning of the world to the resurrection of Christ, was the last day of the week; and, from the resurrection of Christ, was changed into the first day of the week, which, in Scripture, is called the Lord's Day, and is to be continued to the end of the world, as the Christian Sabbath (WCF, chapter 21:7).

So why do we worship as a people on Sunday, and not Saturday? There are several reasons for this. First, in the New Testament we learn that the first day of the week, the day after the Sabbath, is called "the Lord's day" (Rev 1:10 cf. 1 Cor 16:2). This grammatical phrase means that this day especially belongs to our Lord Jesus Christ.

Second, Sunday was the day on which our Lord rose from the dead (John 20:1). The psalmist anticipated Christ's resurrection in saying, "This is the day that the Lord has made; let us rejoice and be glad in it" (Ps 118:24). Sunday is the day of joyful celebration of the living Savior of the world. As St. John of Damascus wrote:

> Now let the heaven be joyful, let earth her song begin;
> Let all the world keep triumph, and all that is therein;
> In grateful exultation their notes let all things blend,
> For Christ the Lord hath risen, our Joy that hath no end.[1]

---

1. Psalter Hymnal, #364.

Third, just as on the first day of creation God made light and separated it from the darkness, we gather on the first day of the week to celebrate the light of the gospel in Jesus Christ, who has separated us from the world of the darkness of sin (John 1:5, 9, 3:19, 8:12; 2 Cor 4:1–6).

Fourth, the particular Old Covenant strictness of the Sabbath law has ceased with the coming of Christ (Col 2:16–17; Gal 4:9–10; Rom 14:5–6). From creation until Christ the people of God worked six days and then rested on the seventh day, looking forward to the day of rest. This was typological of their looking forward to eternal rest. From the advent of Christ until his coming again the people of God rest on the first day and work the next six, looking back on the finished work of Christ. When our Lord lay in the tomb from Friday evening through early Sunday morning, the old order of things was buried with him; and when he rose again he began a new order of things. This is why the Gospel of John speaks of the first day of the week as the eighth day, literally, "after eight days" (20:26). It was not just the beginning of another week, but in fact, a new beginning. The Epistle of Barnabus (ca. 100) spoke of this day as the "beginning of another world" that "we keep…with joyfulness" (ch. 15).

The Lord's Day is not to be a burden, for as Jesus himself said, "The Sabbath was made for man, not man for the Sabbath" (Mark 2:27). The prophet Isaiah once said,

> If you turn back your foot from the Sabbath, from doing your pleasure on my holy day, and call the Sabbath a delight and the holy day of the Lord honorable; if you honor it, not going your own ways, or seeking your own pleasure, or talking idly; then you shall take delight in the Lord, and I will make you ride on the heights of the earth; I will feed you with the heritage of Jacob your father, for the mouth of the Lord has spoken" (Isa 58:13–14).

Since it is *the Lord's* Day, it is his will for us that we diligently attend church, "not neglecting to meet together, as is the habit of some, but encouraging one another, and all the more as you see the Day drawing near" (Heb 10:25). This diligence in anticipation of the final Day is seen in the early account of the church, which

"*devoted* themselves to the apostles' teaching and fellowship, to the breaking of bread and the prayers" (Acts 2:42).

MORNING & EVENING

Instead of seeing the Lord's Day as a rule that stifles our "weekend," we need to view it as a gift from God that actually structures our lives by providing a rhythm to keep the Lord's Day. The practice of the Lord's Day is not legalism, but it is a part of our piety, that is, our grateful response to God's gifts. We sanctify the day because we ultimately belong not to this age that is passing away, but to the glorious age to come: "our citizenship is in heaven" (Phil 3:20).

Therefore, we gather as a community in the morning and evening on the Lord's Day. We acknowledge that Sunday is the Lord's Day and not the Lord's morning (or sadly for so many, the Lord's hour), just as the Sabbath was a day of rest. The Reformation churches followed the historic practice of the ancient Christian church in worshipping twice on the Lord's Day as a practical way of keeping it "holy" (Exod 20:8; Deut 5:12).

This pattern of the day of rest being structured at each end with morning and evening worship is not only the historic pattern of the Christian and Protestant churches, but it is also a basic biblical pattern. In creation, God structured time in terms of evenings and mornings (Gen 1–2), and in the life of his redeemed people, there was to be morning and evening sacrifices and prayers at the tabernacle and temple (Exod 29:38–42; 30:7–8; Lev 6:19; Num 28:3–31; 29:6–38). These sacrifices were interpreted by the biblical writers as the "sacrifice of praise" (Ps 50:14; Heb 13:15; see Mal 3:3–4; 1 Peter 2:4–10). This pattern of morning and evening sacrifices of prayer was especially true on the Sabbath (cf. Ps 92). It is evident all throughout the Psalms (e.g., Pss 1:2; 5:3; 77:6; 141:2), the history of Israel's synagogues, the Book of Acts (Acts 3:1; 10:9), and the history of the Church in what later was called matins and vespers, morning and evening prayers. For example, the ancient Christian document known as the Apostolic Constitutions has a section entitled, "That Every Christian Ought to Frequent the Church Diligently Both

Morning and Evening," as there were services held in the morning and evening every day of the week. On the Lord's Day Christians were to "meet more diligently" (Book 2.7.59).

Just as circumcision, Passover, and the Sabbath of the Old Covenant find their counterpoints in baptism, the Lord's Supper, and the Lord's Day in the New Covenant, so the New Testament teaches that the daily morning and evening sacrifices were fulfilled in the daily public and private prayers of the church. In the book of Acts we learn that the early church gathered at the temple and held public prayer services there as well as in their homes. In Acts 2:42 the members of the church "devoted themselves . . . to the prayers." Then in Acts 2:46 we learn that the believers gathered and prayed in private in their homes, as well (cf. Acts 1:14; 4:23–31; 12:12–17). This is also shown in Paul's words about prayer. When Paul says, for example, to "pray without ceasing"/"continually" (1 Thess 5:17; see Eph 6:18; Heb 13:15; Rom 12:12; 1 Tim 5:5) he is speaking in an Old Testament way. The daily morning and evening sacrifices mentioned above were called the tamid offering, that is, the "regular"/"continual" offerings. This is brought out in the King James/English Standard translations of 2 Timothy 1:3: "I remember you constantly in my prayers night and day" (2 Tim 1:3; see Rom 1:9–10; 1 Cor 1:4; Eph 5:20; Phil 1:4; 4:4–6; Col 1:3; 1 Thess 1:2–3; 2:13; 3:6, 10; 2 Thess 1:3, 11; 2:13; Philem 4). What this means is that Paul is telling us to offer up the "sacrifice of praise" (Heb 13:15), as Israel, in the morning and evening.

We also follow this practice because the elders of the church exercise their Christ-ordained authority for the well being of the church in ordering the Lord's Day in such a way:

> In the mean time we believe though it is useful and ben-
> eficial that those who are rulers of the Church institute
> and establish certain ordinances among themselves for
> maintaining the body of the Church; yet they ought stu-
> diously to take care that they do not depart from those
> things which Christ, our only master, hath instituted.
> And, therefore, we reject all human inventions, and all
> laws which man would introduce into the worship of
> God, thereby to bind and compel the conscience in any

manner whatever. Therefore we admit only of that which tends to nourish and preserve concord and unity, and to keep all men in obedience to God. (BC, article 32)

As those who do not exist for themselves but for the Lord (Rom 14:7), we commit ourselves to setting aside this day for grateful resting and worshipping of the Triune God. The Lord's Day is the day in which Jesus takes us to our Father and places us into his arms and feeds us with the Holy Spirit's food for our souls. There is, then, nothing better we can do on the Lord's Day than assemble as a people to worship our covenant God together and receive his grace. As J. C. Ryle said,

> Never be absent from God's house on Sundays, without good reason, – never to miss the Lord's Supper when administered in our own congregation, – never to let our place be empty when means of grace are going on, this is one way to be a growing and prosperous Christian. The very sermon that we needlessly miss, may contain a precious word in season for our souls. The very assembly for prayer and praise from which we stay away, may be the very gathering that would have cheered, and stablished, and quickened our hearts.[2]

SPECIAL SERVICES

Finally, while we believe service on the Lord's Day to be a biblical *must*, service on other occasions is a matter of Christian freedom (Rom 14:1–12). The elders *may* call services for the congregation on days other than the Lord's Day. Services may be called for times of "solemn fastings, and thanksgivings, upon special occasions . . . in their several times and seasons" (WCF, chapter 21.5). As well, in historic Protestant and Reformed churches, the five "Evangelical Feast Days" are also celebrated. These days upon which the work of Christ for us is celebrated in his birth (Christmas), death (Good

2. J. C. Ryle, Expository Thoughts on John, 454–55.

Friday), resurrection (Easter), ascending into heaven (Ascension), and pouring out of the Holy Spirit (Pentecost).[3]

When we gather, then, it is not merely out of custom or tradition, but for the significant purpose of obeying the command of God to gather around the heavenly mountain one day out of seven, since that is specifically "his day." In doing this, we receive the great blessing of "let[ting] the Lord work in me by His Holy Spirit, and thus begin in this life the eternal Sabbath (HC, Q&A 103).

3. For more on these days see Hyde, "Lutheran Puritanism?", 61–83.

Conclusion

In this brief survey of Reformed worship, I have explained that we exist as image-bearers of the Triune God to worship him. After all, this is what we will do for all eternity as the redeemed multitude that no one can number (Rev 7:9). I have shown you the why, the what, and the when of Reformed worship. I trust in all this you have seen the highest and ultimate source of our faith and life as Reformed churches is Scripture. You and I, though, have only scratched the surface of the significance of service that is pleasing to God. I look forward to continuing the journey of learning with you as we join in the wonder of responding to the Lord's serving us, saying:

> Come, let us sing for joy to the Lord;
> Let us shout aloud to the Rock of our salvation.
> Psalm 95:1 (New International Version)

Appendix
Why Some Pastors Wear a Robe

As I OPENED THIS booklet saying, most of those in my congregation and many other Reformed congregations know by experience that to enter the service of a Reformed church from the plethora of non-denominational churches is a culture shock. There is no praise band but an organ, piano, maybe a simple guitar or two, or even no instruments at all. There may be no overhead projected music but instead the people sing from hymnals or songs printed in a service booklet. The service is not a time of "hanging out with Jesus," but is a formal meeting with God.

There is another difference that I would like address here. It is a difference that is noticed in my congregation, but may not be noticed everywhere. This is why I am making this an appendix. In many Reformed congregations the pastor does not wear a Hawaiian shirt or any other informal attire, but a suit. In the congregation I serve (and other Reformed churches you may experience) I wear a plain black robe while I lead and preach. It is this robe that I would like to explain here.

For many, this looks "Catholic." For others, this looks like we are no different than the pastors in many liberal churches that do not take the Bible seriously, such as the Crystal Cathedral, which you may have seen on Sunday morning television. Because there is this perception, what follows is a basic explanation for why I (and many other Reformed pastors) wear a preaching/pulpit robe, also called "The Genevan Gown."

THE BIBLICAL TEACHING ON OFFICE

The first, and main, reason for this practice is the biblical teaching on office in the Church. The Bible teaches the concept that God has called pastors/ministers to a special office, that is, an official and authoritative function in the life of God's people. One need only read the New Testament epistles to see this. For example, Paul says Christ has given pastors and teachers to the church to build up the saints (Eph 4:11–12). Further, he says elsewhere that "God has appointed in the church . . . apostles . . . prophets . . . teachers," and then asks, "Are all apostles? Are all prophets? Are all teachers?" (1 Cor 12:28–29) Because God places men in specific offices to serve the church, the people of God are to honor, respect, and submit to those officers:

> Obey your leaders and submit to them, for they are keeping watch over your souls, as those who will have to give an account. Let them do this with joy and not with groaning, for that would be of no advantage to you (Heb 13:17).

In light of texts like these, the ancient church father Ignatius of Antioch (*ca.* 50–117), wrote a letter *To the Smyrnaeans*, saying, "See that ye all follow the bishop, even as Jesus Christ does the Father" (ch. 8). He also wrote in his letter *To the Ephesians*, saying, "We should look upon the bishop even as we would upon the Lord Himself" (ch. 6). The reason for Scripture and Ignatius saying this is because of the office of the ministry. This is what Paul so clearly teaches, saying, "We ask you, brothers, to respect those who labor among you and are over you in the Lord and admonish you, and to esteem them very highly in love *because of their work*" (1 Thess 5:12–13).

For some, this might be a challenge if the one in office is a friend, peer, family member, or even one who is younger. Nevertheless, Paul exhorts Timothy, a young pastor, saying, "Let no one despise you for your youth" (1 Tim 4:12) precisely because in this very same chapter Paul calls Timothy a "good servant of Christ Jesus," that is, a minister of Christ (1 Tim 4:6).

Wearing a robe, then, *emphasizes the office of the minister and de-emphasizes the personality of the man in the pulpit.* It is a way of turning the parishioners' attention away from the person and his personality and putting it where it belongs, on the office of the minister who is the spokesman for the Lord. In the words of Dr. D. Martyn Lloyd-Jones, "The gown . . . is a sign of the call, a sign of the fact that a man has been 'set apart' to do this work. It is no more than that, but it is that."[1]

In the Bible, we see that the clothing and calling of those in special offices are often connected. In other words, clothing visually reflects a person's calling or office.[2] The purpose of the robe is to cover the man and accent his God-ordained office or calling before the people of God.

In the Bible, ministers of the Lord have a representative role during the public assembly. When he leads the congregation in prayer before God, he represents Christ leading the church in prayer before the Father. When he reads and preaches the Word, he represents Christ, the Husband, speaking to his holy bride. The robe does not set him *above* the congregation, but sets him *apart* for his office as pastor on the Lord's Day. Better yet, the robe does not set him apart *from* his congregation, but sets him apart *for* his congregation, to do the work to which Christ has called him.

This may seem strange, especially if you are used to "getting to know the man" in the pulpit. There is a time and a place for the minister to get to know his people casually, socially, and intimately, but the time for this is not in the pulpit. In the pulpit, the minister is your minister, who serves the Lord by feeding your soul with spiritual food.

1. Lloyd-Jones, *Preaching and Preachers*, 160.
2. Gen 9:20–27; 39:1–13; 37:3–11, 23; 41:1–44; many references in Exodus and Leviticus; 1 Sam 2:19; 15:27; 18:4; 24:4, 5, 11, 14; Ezra 9:3–5; Esth 8:15; Isa 22:21; Jonah 3:6; Matt 22:11ff.; 27:31; Mark 16:5; Luke 15:22; Rev 1:13; 4:4; 6:11; 19:13, 16.

THE PRACTICE OF CHURCH HISTORY

Another reason I wear a robe is that from the Reformation until very recently, Protestant pastors wore robes of office when serving. The robe, then, *emphasizes that we are a part of the historic Christian Church.*[3]

Some think the preaching robe is too Roman Catholic, though. The fact is, though, that preaching robes did not originate with the Roman Catholic Church, but were worn in the ancient Church. For example, the Synod of Laodicea (*ca.* mid-fourth century] said, "The subdeacon (an order of ministry below the deacon) has no right to wear an *orarium* [a liturgical scarf]" (Canon 22). Another example would be the ancient iconography and art that shows ordained men in distinct dress. Our Protestant forefathers and the later Puritans in England and America all wore preaching garments.

As well, there is a huge difference between a Protestant minister wearing a preaching robe and the priestly garments of Rome. As a Reformed Church, our ministers are preachers and pastors, not priests. The Reformers stopped using the vestments of the priesthood for this reason. In its place, they wore plain, simple, and unadorned black robes while preaching, instead of the elaborate, complex, and overly symbolic garments of the priests. Yet while the special, "holy" liturgical vestments were removed, in their place ministers wore plain liturgical attire. Here is how Martin Bucer, on behalf of all the Protestant ministers of the city of Strasbourg, explained the rationale for this change in 1524:

> . . . in our churches we have completely done away with and abolished everything which has no basis in the Scriptures and which has been added to the Lord's Supper without any justification in the Scriptures and therefore has been an insult and a slander of Christ and of the divine mercies . . . the priest and servant of the congregation does not wear a special vestment, only

---

3. For an excellent summary of the history of vestments see *The Oxford History of Christian Worship*, 841–57.

what we call the choir gown, and none of the sacrificial vestments such as alb, stole, chasuble, etc.[4]

In this same treatise, Bucer devoted an entire chapter to the "Reason Why the Papist [Roman Catholic] Vestments Have Been Abolished." In this chapter, he explained that the example of the high priests in the Old Testaments with all their vestments does not apply, as Rome said of their priesthood. Instead, Bucer said,

> Christ is our High Priest in the line of Aaron . . . His priestly garments, and those of all of us who are united with Him in true faith and therefore are also priests, are not made with hands, but spiritual clothing such as truth, justice and righteousness and all things which are in Christ.[5]

THE CONTEMPORARY CHURCH

The third basic reason why I wear a robe while preaching and leading in worship, is that the pastor is not a businessman of an upper middle class corporation, but a minister of Jesus Christ. Even churches in which the pastor does not wear a robe, there is an expectation that he dress conservatively, with a dark suit, white starched shirt, and conservative necktie. In our culture this is the weekday uniform of a lawyer and businessman. This "uniform" often communicates precisely the wrong message to the church and community in which we minister. We do not derive our authority from the symbols of our culture, but from Christ and his Word.

The culture also pulls us to the other extreme of informality. After wearing business suits and office attire all week, we all too often want to come to church and relax. Instead, the robe *emphasizes that we do not identify ourselves to the spirit of the age.* It focuses the congregation on the work of Christ and apostolic doctrine—which transcend all cultures. For those who cannot afford a suit or even a

4. Cypris, *Basic Principles*, I, 2.
5. Cypris, *Basic Principles*, V, 68.

nice Sunday outfit the robe is neutral and says, "We are Christians here, not upper-middle class Americans."

Therefore, in wearing a robe, I am practicing something consistent with what the Bible teaches about office, what the historic Church has practiced, and what Protestants have done for five hundred years. I am also taking a stance against the American church's tendency to turn the pastor into an executive or an informal friend.

Bibliography

Castleman, Robbie. *Parenting in the Pew*. Downers Grove: Inter-Varsity Press, 1993.

Clarkson, David. "Public Worship to be Prefered Before Private." In *The Works of David Clarkson*, 3 vols., 3.187–209. 1864, repr., Edinburgh: Banner of Truth, 1988.

Cypris, Ottoman Frederick. *Basic Principles: Translation and Comentary on Martin Bucer's Grund und Ursach*, 1524. Th.D diss., Theological Seminary of New York, 1971.

Hyde, Daniel R. "According to the Custom of the Ancient Church? Examining the Roots of John Calvin's Liturgy." *Puritan Reformed Journal* 1:2 (June 2009) 189–211.

———. *In Defense of the Descent: A Response to Contemporary Critics*. Grand Rapids: Reformation Heritage Books, 2010.

———. *In Living Color: Images of Christ and the Means of Grace*. Grandville: Reformed Fellowship, 2009.

———. *Jesus Loves the Little Children: Why We Baptize Children*. 2006; Grandville: Reformed Fellowship, second edition 2012)

———. "Lift Up Your Hearts: Increasing the Use of the Sursum Corda." *Reformed Worship* 82 (December 2006) 33–35.

———. "Lost Keys: The Absolution in Reformed Liturgy." *Calvin Theological Journal* 46:1 (April 2011) 140–66.

———. "Lutheran Puritanism? Adiaphora in Lutheran Orthodoxy and Possible Commonalities in Reformed Orthodoxy." *American Theological Inquiry* 2:1 (January 2009) 61–83.

———. *Welcome to a Reformed Church: A Guide for Pilgrims*. Orlando: Reformation Trust Publishing, 2010.

Lloyd-Jones, D. Martyn. *Preaching and Preachers*. Grand Rapids: Zondervan, 1971.

Psalter Hymnal. Grand Rapids: Christian Reformed Church, 1976.

Ryle, J. C. *Expository Thoughts on John: Volume 3*. 1873; Edinburgh: Banner of Truth, reprinted 1999.

Sing! a new creation. Grand Rapids: CRC Publications, 2001.

The Oxford History of Christian Worship, ed. Geoffrey Wainwright and Karen B. Westfield Tucker. New York: Oxford University Press, 2006.

Trinity Hymnal. 1990; Atlanta: Great Commission Publications, fourth printing 1994.